I Like Storybooks

by
Liliana Santirso and Martha Avilés

HARCOURT BRACE & COMPANY

Orlando Atlanta Austin Boston San Francisco Chicago Dallas New York
Toronto London

This edition is published by special arrangement with CELTA Amaquemecan.

English translation copyright © 1994 by Harcourt Brace & Company

Grateful acknowledgment is made to CELTA Amaquemecan for permission to reprint *I Like Storybooks* by Liliana Santirso, illustrated by Martha Avilés. Text © 1991 by Liliana Santirso; illustrations © 1991 by Martha Avilés. Originally published in Spanish under the title *Me gustan los libros de cuentos*, Amecameca, Mexico.

Printed in the United States of America

ISBN 0-15-302124-1

4 5 6 7 8 9 10   035   97 96 95

I Like Storybooks

by
Liliana Santirso and Martha Avilés

I like storybooks!
They know the secrets of people and
animals, both real and make-believe.

Every book is a door
that opens to a different world.

With books, I can fly through space

and through time.

I can be another child, in another home, in a different school.

I can become a brave hero

or fight with pirates.

I can get away from animals
that want to eat me

and come back just in time
to have my milk and cookies.

So when I pick up a storybook,
I put on my seat belt

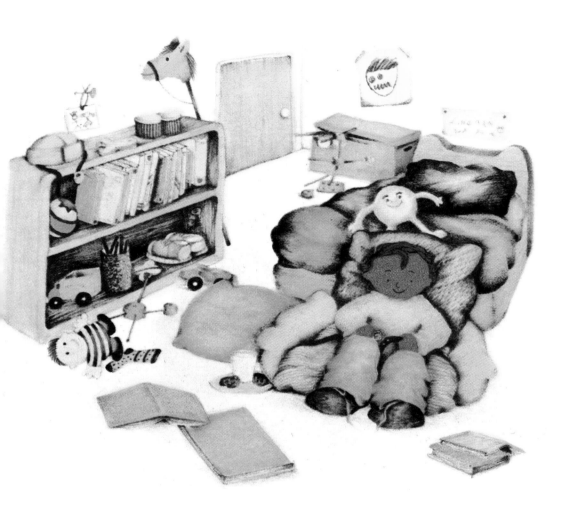

and hold on real tight!

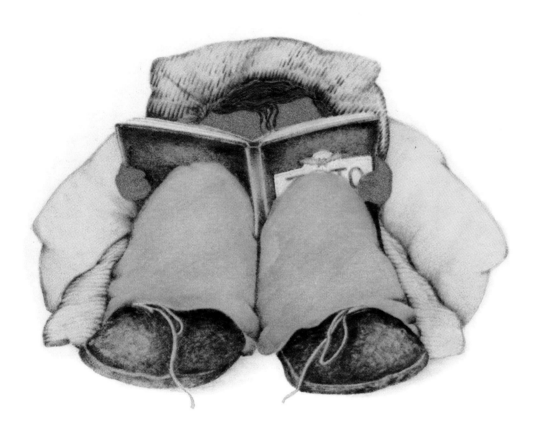